Edge of Excellence

Mastering the Psychological Game in Sports

Freudian Trips

Copyright Page

© 2023 by Freudian Trips

This book is a work of non-fiction. Unless otherwise noted, the author and the publisher make no explicit guarantees as to the accuracy of the information contained in this book and will not be held responsible for any errors or omissions.

Published by Omniterra Media Inc

First Edition

Visit the author's website at www.freudiantrips.com

Disclaimer

The views and opinions expressed in this book are those of the author(s) and do not necessarily reflect the official policy or position of any other agency, organization, employer, or company. The contents of this book are for informational and educational purposes only and are not intended to serve as professional advice, diagnosis, or treatment.

The information provided in this book is believed to be accurate and reliable as of the date of publication. However, it may include some errors or inaccuracies, and no warranty or guarantee is provided regarding the accuracy, timeliness, or applicability of the content.

Readers are encouraged to consult with professional philosophers, educators, or other qualified professionals where appropriate for personalized advice. The author(s) and publisher shall not be liable for any loss, damage, or harm caused or alleged to be caused, directly or indirectly, by the information or ideas contained, suggested, or referenced in this book.

By reading this book, the reader acknowledges and agrees that they are solely responsible for how they interpret and apply the information contained herein.

This book may also include references to other works, studies, and sources. These references are provided for further reading and exploration and do not imply endorsement or validation of the specific theories, viewpoints, or interpretations presented in those works.

Chapter 1: The Synergy of Mind and Muscle: Unveiling the World of Sports Psychology

The Fusion of Psychology and Physicality in Sports

Welcome to the intriguing world where the mind meets muscle - the realm of sports psychology. Often, when we think of sports, images of physical prowess, endurance, and skill come to mind. However, there's another side to this athletic coin - the psychological aspect. Sports aren't just a test of physical abilities; they're also a mental marathon. Imagine a sprinter at the starting blocks or a golfer poised for a swing; it's not just their bodies at work, but also their minds, laser-focused and strategizing. This chapter aims to explore this blend of mental and physical elements in sports, illustrating how psychological factors like confidence, focus, and motivation can be as crucial as physical training.

Exploring the Essence of Sports Psychology

Sports psychology studies how psychological variables impact physical performance as well as how psychological and physical variables are impacted by engaging in physical activity and sports. It's a discipline that helps athletes enhance their performance, recover from injuries, and deal with the pressures of competition. But it's not just for elite athletes; it applies to anyone who participates in sports or physical activity. This field explores various aspects like motivation - what drives an athlete to push through pain and fatigue, the anxiety and stress of competition, and the significance of mental well-being in physical performance.

To understand sports psychology, imagine your mind as a powerful tool that can either propel you to victory or hinder your performance. It's about harnessing this power to optimize performance. For instance, a basketball player might use visualization techniques to imagine making the perfect shot, or a runner might use self-talk to push through the last mile of a marathon. These mental strategies are as integral to sports as physical training.

Aim and Framework of the Book

This book is designed as a guide to the fascinating world of sports psychology, intended for athletes, coaches, students, and sports enthusiasts. Whether you're a weekend warrior, a budding young athlete, or a coach, understanding the principles of sports psychology can enhance your approach to sports and exercise. This chapter sets the stage for the rest of the book, which will dive into various topics like mental toughness, motivation, focus, and handling pressure. Each subsequent chapter will offer insights and practical strategies to apply the principles of sports psychology in your athletic endeavors or everyday life.

Our journey through this book will be both educational and practical. We'll explore theories and research, but we'll also provide real-world applications and exercises. By the end of this book, you'll have a deeper understanding of how the mind influences physical performance and how you can apply these principles to reach your full athletic potential or simply enjoy your sports and fitness activities more fully.

Chapter 2: The Athlete's Psyche - Understanding and Overcoming Mental Hurdles

Welcome to a journey into the minds of athletes, where mental fortitude is as crucial as physical strength. This chapter delves into the psychological makeup of athletes, unraveling the mental challenges they face and exploring strategies to overcome them. Our goal is to provide insight that's accessible and engaging for everyone, from seasoned athletes to sports enthusiasts.

Psychological Makeup of an Athlete

At the heart of every athlete is a unique blend of mental traits that drive their performance. These include:

Resilience: The ability to bounce back from setbacks, be it a loss, an injury, or a bad performance. Resilient athletes view challenges as opportunities to learn and grow.

Focus: The capacity to concentrate on the task at hand while blocking out distractions. A focused athlete can maintain attention on their goals, whether during a high-pressure game or a routine training session.

Motivation: The internal drive that propels athletes towards their goals. This can stem from a love for the sport, the thrill of competition, or personal ambitions.

Confidence: Belief in one's abilities is crucial. Confident athletes trust their training and skills, which enables them to perform at their best.

Mental Toughness: This is the ability to persevere through difficult situations and remain determined and focused. Mental toughness helps athletes endure the demands of their sport.

Understanding these traits helps us appreciate the psychological complexities athletes navigate in their pursuit of excellence.

Mental Challenges and Overcoming Them

Athletes, like all of us, face a range of mental challenges. Here, we explore some common ones and how they can be overcome:

Dealing with Pressure: Athletes often face immense pressure to perform, which can lead to anxiety and stress. Overcoming this involves techniques like deep breathing, mindfulness, and positive self-talk to maintain calm and focus.

Overcoming Fear of Failure: Fear of failure can be paralyzing. Athletes can combat this by setting realistic goals, focusing on the process rather than just the outcome, and viewing failures as learning opportunities.

Maintaining Motivation: Motivation can wane, especially in the face of obstacles. Setting short-term, achievable goals, remembering the reasons why they started the sport, and celebrating small victories can help maintain motivation.

Building Confidence: Confidence can fluctuate. Athletes build it by focusing on their strengths, learning from mistakes, and visualizing successful outcomes.

Handling Setbacks: Injuries or losses are inevitable. The key to overcoming them lies in accepting the situation, focusing on recovery or learning from losses, and setting new, achievable targets.

These mental challenges are not insurmountable. By understanding and applying psychological strategies, athletes can overcome these hurdles and enhance their performance.

Chapter 3: Cultivating Resilience and Grit - The Art of Bouncing Back

In the arena of sports, and indeed in life, resilience and grit are the cornerstones of success. This chapter focuses on developing mental resilience, a crucial skill for athletes and non-athletes alike. We will explore what resilience and grit are, why they matter, and provide practical strategies to strengthen them.

Developing Mental Resilience

What is Mental Resilience?

Mental resilience refers to the ability to adapt to challenges, stress, and adversity. It's not about avoiding problems or not feeling the pressure; it's about facing these challenges head-on and emerging stronger.

Why is it Important?

In sports, as in life, things don't always go as planned. Injuries, defeats, and unexpected setbacks are part of the journey. Resilience is what allows athletes to navigate these challenges without losing confidence or motivation.

How to Develop It

Embrace Challenges: Start viewing challenges as opportunities to learn rather than obstacles. This shift in mindset is the first step towards building resilience.

Stay Positive: Maintaining a positive attitude helps in coping with tough situations. This doesn't mean ignoring problems, but rather focusing on solutions and learning from experiences.

Build a Support System: Surround yourself with people who encourage and support you. This network can be coaches, teammates, family, or friends.

Take Care of Your Body and Mind: Regular exercise, a healthy diet, and adequate rest are crucial. Mental and physical health are deeply interconnected.

Learn Stress Management Techniques: Practices such as mindfulness, meditation, and deep breathing exercises can help manage stress effectively.

Strategies for Bouncing Back from Defeat

Understanding Defeat

Defeat is not a sign of weakness; it's an inevitable part of growth. It's important to understand that even the greatest athletes have faced defeat at some point in their careers.

Strategies to Overcome Defeat

Acknowledge Your Feelings: It's okay to feel disappointed or upset. Acknowledge these feelings, but don't dwell on them.

Analyze and Learn: Reflect on what went wrong and what you can learn from it. This process can turn a loss into a valuable learning experience.

Set New Goals: Redirect your focus towards new, achievable goals. This helps maintain motivation and gives a sense of direction.

Stay Committed to Your Routine: Consistency in training and preparation builds discipline and resilience. Stick to your routines, even when it feels tough.

Seek Feedback: Constructive feedback from coaches, mentors, or peers can provide valuable insights on areas of improvement.

Resilience and grit are not innate traits; they are skills that can be developed over time. By embracing challenges, maintaining a positive outlook, and learning from defeats, you can cultivate these qualities. Remember, resilience is about how you respond to the hurdles on your path. The ability to bounce back stronger is what separates good athletes from great ones. This chapter is your guide to building the mental toughness that will not only aid in sports but will also enrich your life in countless ways.

Chapter 4: Achieving the Optimal Performance State - Entering and Sustaining the 'Flow'

Welcome to Chapter 4, where we dive into the concept of achieving the optimal performance state in sports and in life. This chapter is dedicated to understanding what "flow" is and how one can reach and maintain this state of peak performance.

Understanding and Achieving the "Flow"

What is the "Flow"?

"Flow" is a term used to describe a state of complete immersion and focus in an activity. When you're in the flow, you're fully engaged, time seems to stand still, and everything else fades away. It's often described by athletes as being "in the zone."

Why is Flow Important?

Achieving flow is crucial for peak performance. It's a state where skills are used to their fullest, leading to exceptional performance. Athletes in flow often perform effortlessly and with great enjoyment.

How to Achieve Flow

Find Your Passion: Flow is more likely to occur in activities you are passionate about. Determine what you enjoy doing, then put all of your energy into it.

Balance Challenge and Skill: Flow happens when the challenge of an activity matches your skill level. Too easy, and you'll get bored; too hard, and you'll get frustrated.

Set Clear Goals: Having specific, achievable goals for each session or competition helps focus your attention and gives you a sense of direction.

Eliminate Distractions: Create an environment where you can concentrate fully. This might mean finding a quiet space, turning off your phone, or practicing mindfulness.

Practice Regularly: The more you practice, the more familiar and skilled you become at an activity, increasing your chances of entering flow.

Methods to Sustain Peak Performance

What is Peak Performance?

Peak performance is the ability to perform at the highest level of your capability. It involves optimal functioning, where physical and mental abilities are fully tapped.

How to Sustain Peak Performance

Consistent Practice: Regular and deliberate practice is key. It helps refine your skills and keeps you prepared for high-level performance.

Physical Fitness: Maintain a high level of physical fitness. A strong, healthy body supports a strong mind.

Mental Preparation: Techniques like visualization, where you imagine yourself succeeding, can prepare your mind for peak performance.

Recovery and Rest: Balance hard work with adequate rest. Recovery is essential to prevent burnout and sustain high performance levels.

Healthy Lifestyle: Eating well, staying hydrated, and getting enough sleep are crucial. A healthy lifestyle supports both physical and mental well-being.

Adaptability: Be ready to adapt your strategies as needed. Flexibility in approach allows you to maintain peak performance even when conditions change.

Achieving and sustaining the flow and peak performance is a journey. It's about finding the right balance between challenge and skill, setting clear goals, eliminating distractions, and being consistent in your practice. Remember, this state is as much about mental preparation and well-being as it is about physical fitness and skill. By applying these principles, you can maximize your potential in sports and enjoy the rewarding experience of being in the zone. This chapter is your guide to unlocking that optimal performance state, a state where your abilities, focus, and enjoyment align perfectly.

Chapter 5: Mastery of Focus - Enhancing Attention and Coping with Distractions

In sports and in life, the ability to focus is a powerful tool. This chapter is dedicated to understanding how to enhance your attention and concentration, and how to effectively manage distractions, both external and internal.

Enhancing Attention and Concentration

What is Focus?

Focus in sports refers to the ability to direct your attention to the task at hand while ignoring other, less important things. It's like shining a spotlight on what really matters in the moment.

Why is Focus Important?

Your ability to focus can make the difference between a good performance and a great one. When you're fully focused, your execution becomes more precise, your reactions quicker, and your awareness heightened.

How to Enhance Your Focus

Practice Mindfulness: Mindfulness is about being present in the moment. Techniques like mindful breathing or meditation can train your brain to focus better.

Set Specific Goals: Before you start an activity, set clear, achievable goals. This helps your mind lock onto specific objectives.

Create a Pre-Performance Routine: Develop a routine that helps you get into the right mindset. This could be a series of stretches, a particular warm-up, or even a mental checklist.

Break Tasks into Smaller Segments: Large tasks can be overwhelming. Breaking them down into smaller, manageable parts can help maintain focus.

Train in Different Environments: Practicing in various settings can improve your ability to maintain focus amid changing conditions.

Coping with External and Internal Distractions

Types of Distractions

Distractions can be external, like noise from a crowd, or internal, like your own thoughts or feelings.

Managing External Distractions

Control What You Can: Minimize distractions in your environment when possible. For example, if you're easily distracted by noise, using earplugs during training might help.

Desensitize Yourself: Train in environments similar to where you'll compete. This can help you get used to potential distractions.

Refocus Quickly: Develop a habit of quickly bringing your focus back when you notice it drifting.

Managing Internal Distractions

Acknowledge and Redirect: Recognize when your thoughts are drifting. Acknowledge these thoughts and then gently redirect your focus back to the task.

Positive Self-talk: Replace negative thoughts with positive affirmations. This can help keep self-doubt and anxiety at bay.

Visualize Success: Regularly visualize yourself performing successfully. This practice can help keep your thoughts aligned with your goals.

Mastering focus is not just about eliminating distractions but learning to direct your attention where it's most needed. By practicing mindfulness, setting clear goals, developing a pre-performance routine, and learning to manage distractions, you can significantly enhance your ability to focus. Remember, focus is a skill, and like any skill, it gets better with practice. Use this chapter as your guide to sharpening this vital tool in your arsenal, enhancing not just your sports performance but your everyday life activities as well.

Chapter 6: Fueling the Desire to Excel - Understanding and Nurturing Motivation

This chapter delves into the core of what drives us to do better, to push further, and to reach higher: motivation. We will explore the dynamics of internal and external motivation and discuss how to inspire both oneself and others, particularly in a team setting.

Dynamics of Internal and External Motivation

Understanding Motivation

Motivation is the force that drives you to act. It's the difference between waking up before dawn to train and hitting the snooze button. In the realm of sports and beyond, motivation is a key player in the pursuit of excellence.

Types of Motivation

Internal Motivation: This comes from within. It's driven by personal satisfaction, enjoyment, and the desire to achieve. An internally motivated athlete might play a sport because they genuinely love it, not just to win medals.

External Motivation: This type involves outside rewards or pressures, like trophies, social recognition, or avoiding negative consequences. An externally motivated athlete might train hard to win a championship or to gain approval from others.

Balancing Internal and External Motivation

The most effective motivation often combines both internal and external elements. For example, an athlete might be driven by a love for their sport (internal) and the desire to win a competition (external).

Inspiring Oneself and Team Dynamics

Self-Motivation Strategies

Set Personal Goals: These should be challenging yet achievable. Setting goals gives you a clear target to aim for.

Celebrate Small Victories: Recognizing and celebrating small achievements can boost your morale and keep you motivated.

Find Your Why: Understanding why you're doing something can fuel your drive. Reflect on what drew you to your sport or activity in the first place.

Stay Positive: A positive mindset can keep the flames of motivation burning, even when things get tough.

Motivating a Team

Create a Supportive Environment: A team that supports each other is more likely to stay motivated.

Set Team Goals: Just like personal goals, team goals provide a common target for everyone to strive towards.

Recognize Individual Contributions: Celebrating the achievements of individual team members can boost morale and motivation for the entire group.

Encourage Open Communication: A team where members can openly discuss their ideas and concerns is more cohesive and motivated.

Motivation, both internal and external, is a complex but vital element in the pursuit of excellence. Understanding what drives you and how to harness these forces can significantly impact your performance and enjoyment in sports. For team settings, fostering a motivating environment involves not just focusing on the collective goal but also recognizing and nurturing the individual aspirations and contributions of each team member. This chapter is your guide to unlocking and maintaining the desire to excel, a journey that is as personal as it is universal.

Chapter 7: Setting Goals and Reaching Them - Charting the Path to Success

In this chapter, we focus on one of the most crucial aspects of personal and athletic growth: setting goals and achieving them. In this chapter, we will explore effective strategies for setting goals and methods to monitor progress, ensuring that the drive and determination remain strong throughout your journey.

Effective Goal-Setting Strategies

The Importance of Setting Goals

Goals are like the map for your journey. They give you direction and end points to strive for. Without clear goals, it's easy to lose your way or lose sight of what you're working towards.

How to Set Effective Goals

Be Specific: Clear, specific goals are more effective than vague ones. Instead of saying, "I want to get better," say, "I want to improve my time by 30 seconds."

Make Them Measurable: You should be able to measure whether or not you've achieved your goal. For instance, "I want to increase my batting average by 10 points."

Ensure They're Achievable: While it's good to be ambitious, your goals should also be realistic and attainable.

Be Relevant: Your goals should be relevant to your overall aspirations and values.

Time-Bound: Set a timeframe for your goals. This creates a sense of urgency and helps in planning.

Monitoring Progress and Keeping the Drive Alive

Keeping Track of Your Progress

Monitoring your progress is vital for staying on track and maintaining motivation. It helps you see how far you've come and what needs more attention.

Methods to Monitor Progress

Keep a Journal: Documenting your training, thoughts, and feelings can provide insights into your progress and challenges.

Regular Check-ins: Periodically review your goals and assess where you stand in relation to them.

Seek Feedback: Regular feedback from coaches, mentors, or peers can provide an external perspective on your progress.

Maintaining Motivation

Staying motivated, especially in the face of challenges, is crucial for achieving your goals.

Strategies to Keep Motivation High

Celebrate Small Wins: Acknowledge and celebrate the small milestones along the way to your bigger goals.

Remind Yourself of the Bigger Picture: When you feel your motivation waning, remind yourself of why you set these goals in the first place.

Adjust Goals as Needed: Be flexible. If you find a goal is unrealistic, adjust it. Don't view this as failure but as a smart strategy.

Find a Support System: Surround yourself with people who support and believe in you. This can be a significant source of motivation.

Setting and achieving goals is not just about the end result; it's about the journey. Effective goal-setting and maintaining the drive to reach them are skills that will not only aid in your sports endeavors but also in various aspects of life. This chapter provides a roadmap for setting your goals and the tools to help you navigate the path to achieving them. Remember, the process of striving towards your goals is where growth and learning occur. Let this chapter be your guide to setting goals that challenge, inspire, and propel you forward.

Chapter 8: The Power of Visualization - Harnessing Mental Imagery for Athletic Success

Welcome to a journey into the fascinating world of visualization, a powerful tool in an athlete's mental toolkit. This chapter will explore the role and effectiveness of mental imagery in sports and share inspiring success stories from the athletic world.

The Role and Effectiveness of Mental Imagery

What is Visualization?

Visualization, or mental imagery, involves creating or recreating an experience in the mind. In the context of sports, it means picturing yourself performing a task, from running a race to executing a perfect dive, all within your mind's eye.

Why is Visualization Effective?

Visualization works on the principle that the mind can't distinguish well between a vividly imagined experience and a real one. When you visualize yourself performing an action, your brain sends signals to the muscles involved in that action, similar to when you physically perform it. This mental practice can enhance confidence, improve focus, and prepare you for actual performance.

How to Practice Visualization

Find a Quiet Space: Start by finding a quiet, comfortable place where you won't be disturbed.

Relax: Take some deep breaths, relax your body, and clear your mind of distractions.

Create a Vivid Image: Picture the scenario in as much detail as possible – the environment, the sounds, the sensations.

Include Emotions: Imagine the emotions you would feel during the actual performance – the excitement, the adrenaline rush, the satisfaction of a well-executed move.

Repeat: Regular practice is key. The more you visualize, the more effective it becomes.

Success Stories from the Athletic World

Visualization isn't just a theoretical concept; it's a practice used by many top athletes.

Notable Examples

Michael Phelps: The most decorated Olympian of all time, Phelps used visualization extensively. His coach Bob Bowman encouraged him to visualize not only perfect races but also scenarios where things went wrong, so he could be prepared for any situation.

Lindsey Vonn: The Olympic gold-medalist skier used visualization to overcome fears and injuries. She would visualize her ski races, every turn and jump, to ensure she was mentally prepared.

Muhammad Ali: The legendary boxer used mental rehearsals before his fights. He would visualize winning rounds, which helped build his confidence and focus.

Visualization is a powerful mental tool that can enhance athletic performance. It's about more than just seeing yourself succeed; it's about fully immersing yourself in a successful experience, mentally and emotionally. This chapter provides insights into how visualization works and offers real-life examples of its effectiveness. Whether you're an athlete looking to improve your game, a coach aiming to enhance your team's performance, or just someone interested in the power of the mind, understanding and applying the principles of visualization can open doors to new levels of performance and achievement.

Chapter 9: Embracing Mindfulness and Calm - Integrating Inner Peace into Athletic Training

In this chapter, we explore the serene yet powerful world of mindfulness and calm. This chapter is dedicated to understanding how incorporating mindfulness into training regimes can enhance athletic performance and discussing techniques for relaxation and mental recovery.

Incorporating Mindfulness in Training Regimes

Understanding Mindfulness

Mindfulness is the practice of being fully present and engaged in the moment, aware of your thoughts and feelings without distraction or judgment. In the context of sports, it means being completely absorbed in the training or competition, tuned into your body's movements, and mentally clear and focused.

Why Incorporate Mindfulness?

Mindfulness can reduce stress, improve concentration, and enhance overall well-being, which are crucial for optimal athletic performance. It helps athletes stay centered, manage nerves, and perform under pressure.

How to Incorporate Mindfulness into Training

Start with Short Sessions: Begin with 5-10 minutes of mindfulness practice each day and gradually increase the duration.

Mindful Breathing: Focus on your breath, noticing the sensation of air moving in and out of your body. This can be a calming anchor during high-pressure moments.

Body Scan Exercise: Pay attention to different parts of your body, noticing any sensations or tensions. This can help in developing a deeper awareness of your physical state.

Mindful Movement: Practice being mindful during physical activities. Focus on the movement of your body, the rhythm of your steps, or the feeling of your muscles working.

Incorporate into Routine Training: Dedicate a portion of your training sessions to mindfulness exercises, making it a regular part of your regimen.

Techniques for Relaxation and Mental Recovery

Importance of Relaxation and Recovery

Relaxation and mental recovery are as important as physical training. They allow the mind and body to rest, reduce the risk of burnout, and improve overall performance.

Relaxation Techniques

Deep Breathing: Practice deep, slow breathing to calm the mind and reduce tension.

Progressive Muscle Relaxation: Tense and then relax different muscle groups in your body, progressing from your feet up to your head.

Visualization for Relaxation: Imagine a peaceful scene, like a quiet beach or a tranquil forest. Engage all your senses in this visualization to enhance the relaxation experience.

Mindful Meditation: Sit quietly and focus on your breath, a word, or a phrase. If your mind wanders, gently bring it back to your focus point.

Mental Recovery Techniques

Adequate Sleep: Ensure you get enough sleep, as it's essential for mental recovery and overall health.

Digital Detox: Spend some time away from screens and digital devices to give your mind a break.

Engage in Non-Sport Activities: Participate in hobbies or activities outside of your sport to maintain a balanced life and mental state.

Reflection and Journaling: Reflect on your training and competitions. Writing in a journal can help process your thoughts and feelings.

Embracing mindfulness and calm in your training regime can transform your athletic performance. It's about finding balance, staying present, and nurturing both your mind and body. This chapter provides practical strategies to integrate mindfulness into your training and to master the art of relaxation and mental recovery. Whether you're an athlete, coach, or someone looking to improve focus and reduce stress in your life, these techniques can offer significant benefits, helping you perform at your best, both on and off the field.

Chapter 10: Managing Stress and Competitive Anxiety - Strategies for Peak Performance Under Pressure

Welcome to a crucial segment of our journey that addresses a common yet often unspoken challenge in sports and life: managing stress and competitive anxiety. This chapter will provide practical strategies for handling performance anxiety and techniques to excel in high-pressure situations.

Strategies for Handling Performance Anxiety

Understanding Performance Anxiety

Performance anxiety, often known as "stage fright" in sports, is the nervousness or tension an athlete feels before or during a performance. It's a natural response to high-stakes or high-pressure situations, but if not managed, it can negatively impact performance.

Techniques to Manage Performance Anxiety

Preparation and Practice: Being well-prepared through consistent practice can boost your confidence and reduce anxiety.

Deep Breathing Exercises: Deep, controlled breathing can help calm your nervous system and reduce the physical symptoms of anxiety.

Positive Self-talk: Replace negative thoughts with positive affirmations. Remind yourself of your training and past successes.

Visualization: Imagine yourself performing successfully. This mental rehearsal can increase your confidence and decrease anxiety.

Routine Development: Establish a pre-performance routine or ritual. This familiar process can provide comfort and focus before a competition.

Focus on What You Can Control: Concentrate on your performance, not the outcome. Focusing on factors outside your control can heighten anxiety.

Excelling in High-Pressure Situations

Embracing Pressure as an Opportunity

High-pressure situations are often seen as obstacles, but they can also be opportunities to showcase your skills and hard work. Changing your perspective on pressure can transform it from a stressor to a motivator.

Strategies to Excel Under Pressure

Stay in the Present: Focus on the current moment, not past mistakes or future outcomes. Staying present helps keep your mind from wandering to anxiety-inducing thoughts.

Controlled Breathing: Use breathing techniques to maintain calm and focus. For example, try inhaling for four counts, holding for four counts, and exhaling for four counts.

Set Process Goals: Instead of focusing solely on winning, set goals related to your performance, like maintaining a certain technique or strategy.

Embrace the Challenge: View high-pressure situations as challenges to be met rather than threats to be feared.

Practice Under Pressure: Simulate high-pressure scenarios in your training. This can prepare you for the real thing and make you more comfortable when it occurs.

Seek Support: Don't hesitate to talk to coaches, psychologists, or peers about your feelings. Sometimes, just talking about your anxiety can lessen its power.

Managing stress and competitive anxiety is a skill that, like physical training, can be developed and refined. By understanding the nature of performance anxiety and implementing strategies to manage it, you can transform your experience of high-pressure situations from one of fear and apprehension to one of excitement and opportunity. This chapter aims to equip you with the tools needed to navigate the mental and emotional aspects of competition, enabling you to perform at your best when it matters most. Remember, the greatest athletes are not those who never feel anxiety; they are those who have learned to channel it into their performance.

Chapter 11: Psychological Approaches to Injury and Recovery - Navigating the Mental Landscape of Healing

In this chapter, we turn our focus to a critical aspect of sports that affects athletes at all levels: dealing with injuries and the subsequent recovery process. Here, we'll explore strategies to manage the mental impact of injuries and discuss psychological tactics that can aid in an effective and holistic recovery process.

Dealing with the Mental Impact of Injuries

Understanding the Psychological Impact

Injuries are not just physical setbacks; they also carry a significant psychological burden. Athletes might experience a range of emotions, from denial and anger to sadness and anxiety. The sudden disruption of routine, loss of progress, and uncertainty about the future can be mentally challenging.

Strategies to Manage the Emotional Fallout

Acknowledge Your Feelings: It's normal to feel upset or frustrated. Acknowledging these feelings is the first step towards managing them.

Stay Engaged with Your Sport: If possible, stay involved in your team or training environment in some capacity. This can help maintain a sense of connection and purpose.

Set Realistic Goals: Setting small, achievable goals throughout your recovery can provide a sense of progress and accomplishment.

Seek Support: Don't hesitate to talk to a mental health professional, a sports psychologist, or a trusted mentor. Support groups with fellow athletes who have gone through similar experiences can also be beneficial.

Focus on What You Can Control: Direct your energy towards your recovery process and things you can influence, like nutrition and mental health.

Psychological Tactics for Effective Recovery

Adopting a Positive Mindset

A positive mindset can significantly influence the recovery process. Viewing the injury as a temporary setback and focusing on the potential for growth and learning can foster a more constructive approach to recovery.

Tactics to Foster a Positive Recovery Environment

Visualization: Visualize the healing process and eventual return to sport. This can help maintain motivation and a positive outlook.

Develop New Skills: Use the recovery period to develop new skills or interests, both within and outside your sport. This can provide a sense of achievement and diversification.

Practice Mindfulness and Relaxation Techniques: Techniques like deep breathing, meditation, and yoga can aid in reducing stress and promoting a sense of well-being.

Gradual Exposure: As you recover, gradually expose yourself to the sport or activity, building confidence and reducing fear of re-injury.

Maintain a Routine: Establishing a daily routine that includes your rehabilitation exercises, rest, and other activities can provide structure and a sense of normalcy.

Injuries and their recovery are as much a mental journey as they are physical. By understanding and acknowledging the psychological impact of injuries, and employing effective strategies to manage and overcome these challenges, athletes can emerge from the recovery process stronger and more resilient. This chapter provides not just a roadmap for navigating the mental aspects of injury and recovery but also emphasizes the importance of a holistic approach to healing. Remember, an injury is not the end of an athlete's journey; it's a detour that, when navigated thoughtfully, can lead to new paths of growth and understanding.

Conclusion: Integrating Mind and Muscle - The Future of Sports Psychology and Final Inspirations

As we reach the conclusion of our exploration into sports psychology, let's reflect on the key themes and insights we've uncovered. This final chapter aims to bring together the psychological techniques discussed throughout the book, explore the evolving landscape of sports psychology, and leave athletes and coaches with words of inspiration.

Integrating Psychological Techniques in Daily Training

Making Psychology a Routine Practice

Just as physical training is a daily routine for athletes, psychological techniques should also be a regular part of training. Integrating these mental strategies into everyday practice can enhance performance, improve mental well-being, and build a stronger, more resilient athlete.

How to Integrate These Techniques

Start Small: Begin by incorporating simple techniques like mindfulness or positive self-talk into your daily routine.

Make It a Team Effort: Coaches can play a crucial role in integrating these techniques into training sessions, creating a supportive environment for athletes to practice and apply them.

Consistency is Key: Regular practice of psychological techniques is as important as physical training. Make it a non-negotiable part of your daily regimen.

Personalize Your Approach: Each athlete is unique. Encourage athletes to find and adapt techniques that work best for them.

Looking Ahead: The Evolution of Sports Psychology

The Growing Field of Sports Psychology

Sports psychology is a dynamic field, continuously evolving with new research and insights. As our understanding of the human mind deepens, so too will the strategies to optimize athletic performance.

Future Directions

Technological Integration: Advances in technology, like biofeedback and virtual reality, are becoming more prominent in sports psychology, offering new ways to train and enhance mental skills.

Holistic Approach: Athletes' holistic well-being is becoming more and more important, with mental and physical health being equally important.

Accessible Resources: With the rise of digital platforms, psychological training resources are becoming more accessible to athletes at all levels, not just elite performers.

Final Words of Inspiration for Athletes and Coaches

To the Athletes:

Remember, your mind is as powerful a tool as your body. Embrace the psychological aspects of your training with the same vigor as you do the physical. Believe in your capabilities, face challenges with resilience, and never lose sight of your love for the sport. The path to excellence is a journey of both mind and muscle.

To the Coaches:

You have the unique opportunity to shape not just the physical abilities of your athletes but also their mental fortitude. Foster an environment where mental skills are valued and nurtured. Your support and guidance in integrating psychological techniques into training can make a significant difference in your athletes' lives, both in and out of the arena.

In Conclusion:

As we close this book, let's carry forward the understanding that the synergy between the mind and body is the essence of true athletic greatness. The journey of an athlete is not just one of physical prowess but also of mental strength, resilience, and growth. By embracing and integrating the powerful tools of sports psychology, athletes and coaches alike can unlock new levels of performance and personal achievement. Remember, the pursuit of excellence is not just about the medals and records; it's about the journey, the growth, and the indomitable spirit of the athlete.

About Freudian Trips

Welcome to Freudian Trips, your dedicated platform for diving deep into the world of psychology. We are more than just a YouTube channel or a book publisher. We are a beacon of enlightenment, making complex psychological concepts accessible and engaging for all.

Our YouTube channel is a rich repository of psychology made simple. We take the profound and often complex ideas from the world of psychology and break them down into digestible, easy-to-understand content. From the foundational theories of Freud to the cognitive insights of Piaget, we cover a broad spectrum of psychological schools and thoughts, making psychology accessible to everyone, regardless of their background or prior knowledge.

As a book publisher, we take the same approach, transforming intricate psychological theories into comprehensible narratives. Our books are not just collections of words, but vessels of wisdom that make psychology approachable and relatable. We believe that psychology should not be confined to academic circles, but should be available to all who seek to understand the human mind and behavior.

At Freudian Trips, we believe in the power of curiosity and the pursuit of knowledge. We are here to stoke the fires of your curiosity, to guide you on your intellectual journey, and to help you navigate the fascinating world of psychology.

If you are someone who is not afraid to question, to explore, and to learn, then you are in the right place. Join us on this journey of exploration, as we make psychology easy to understand, one concept at a time.

Be sure to visit our Youtube channel at: www.freudiantrips.com/youtube

You can also visit us on the web at www.freudiantrips.com

Welcome to The Freudian Trip community. Stay curious. Stay enlightened.

www.ingramcontent.com/pod-product-compliance
Lightning Source LLC
Chambersburg PA
CBHW071043260726
48661CB00007B/3136